Original title:
Monstera Memories

Copyright © 2025 Creative Arts Management OÜ
All rights reserved.

Author: Fiona Harrington
ISBN HARDBACK: 978-1-80581-883-0
ISBN PAPERBACK: 978-1-80581-410-8
ISBN EBOOK: 978-1-80581-883-0

The Silence Beneath the Canopy

In the shade where shadows dance,
Lurking plants with leafy prance.
Whispers here, a squirrel's debate,
Who knew plants could communicate?

With every rustle, a secret joke,
A fern's smirk, a bamboo's poke.
The roots conspire, an earthy plot,
While I stand still, a baffled spot.

Tales Woven in Verdant Hues

Once a leaf wore a tiny hat,
Claimed it helped him chat with a cat.
A tale so tall, it made me grin,
A lizard laughed, just where to begin?

With creeping vines and stories free,
They plot adventures over tea.
The tales unfold beneath the sun,
Where every plant knows how to run.

Embracing the Jungle Within

Inside my room, a jungle thrives,
With plants that think they're more than vibes.
A cactus pricks with a sharpened quip,
While vines tend to take their own trip.

The ivy giggles, the daisies tease,
Telling stories carried on the breeze.
Yet, here I sit, just trying to write,
While my leafy pals plot their plight.

Serenade of the Sunlit Leaves

Beneath the sun, they sway and sing,
Celebrating all the joy they bring.
A symphony of rustles and sighs,
As petals wink with leafy eyes.

They dance in rhythm, a leafy groove,
Sharing secrets that make me move.
With every twist and lively cheer,
I find their antics hard to steer.

Lush Reflections

In a jungle of green, I lost my hat,
A curious leaf said, "Look at that!"
It danced on a breeze, took off with glee,
As I chased my fashion, it laughed at me.

The vines wrapped around my wayward shoe,
Whispering secrets, laughing, who knew?
I stumbled and fumbled, oh what a sight,
Leaves giggled softly, oh what a plight!

Memories of Tendrils

In the corner, they twist, in the sun's warm glow,
A cast of green actors, putting on a show.
With each little curl, they whisper and sway,
And tell me their jokes in a leafy ballet.

The stories they share, oh so absurd,
Like a plant version of a gossiping bird.
Each vine has a tale, a wild little plot,
Of how they escaped the gardener's knot!

Flora's Embrace

In a tropical hug, I lost track of time,
The leaves chuckled softly, in sync with my rhyme.
With shadows that danced upon wooden floors,
I joined in their fun, like a leaf, I implore!

A party of greenery, spreading their cheer,
Tickling my ankles, "Come join us, dear!"
We spun 'round and twirled, without a care,
In Flora's embrace, laughing, we share.

The Dance of the Leaves

Oh, the leaves they can boogie, it's quite the affair,
They shimmy and shake in the warm summer air.
With a sway and a swirl, they plot and they play,
As I clumsily join them, much to their dismay.

They point at my stumbles, they flick and they flit,
Their laughter so fresh, like a twist of a wit.
Yet I smile and spin, in this leafy delight,
For the dance of the leaves makes everything bright!

Canvas of Living Green

In a house where leaves collide,
A plant danced with a charming stride.
I asked it, "What's your secret, friend?"
It whispered, "Photosynthesis, my trend!"

With sunlight warm it sways with glee,
And shakes its leaves like a jubilee.
I laughed and said, "You're quite the sight!"
"Your green jazz is a pure delight!"

Greenhouse Dreams

In a greenhouse full of leafy cheer,
The plants all gathered, loud and near.
A cactus said, "I need some space!"
While others giggled, rolling with grace.

A fern said, "Just watch me unfurl!"
As vines twirled, with a little whirl.
I joined the party, oh what a scene!
In our little jungle, we reign supreme!

Fronds of the Past

Once in a garden, a tale was spun,
Of fronds that joked and laughed for fun.
A snail came by, slow as could be,
Said, "How do you grow so fabulously?"

The leaves chuckled, swaying with ease,
"With a dash of laughter and a hint of breeze!"
I couldn't help but snort with glee,
In that leafy land, I felt so free!

A Palette of Green Delights

With pots and colors all around,
I stumbled on plants with joy unbound.
A ladybug flashed with a wink,
"My home is here, what do you think?"

The leaves giggled, swaying their way,
Chasing the sun, they danced and played.
I joined in, spreading joy in the light,
In this garden of laughs, everything felt right!

The Palette of Green Memories

In a pot full of leaves, they tell tales,
Whispers of joy in the sun-kissed trails.
Each stem a story, each leaf a laugh,
A garden of giggles in nature's craft.

Dust bunnies dance on the windowsill,
While plants plot pranks with a cheeky thrill.
Cacti poke fun, saying, 'We stand tall!'
While ferns sway softly, 'We've seen it all.'

Unfurling Stories

From tiny seeds to giants, they sprawl,
Telling secrets from the tangible hall.
A leaf rustles, 'Remember the mess?'
As dirt flew high, oh what a process!

Curled up tight, they wait for the play,
Unraveling giggles in leafy ballet.
With each new bud, a jest is born,
As they stretch and yawn, ready to adorn.

Flourishing Memories

Bouncing branches, a jubilant sight,
Swinging and swaying from morning to night.
They laugh at the shadows that dance on the wall,
'This spice of life? Just a botanical brawl!'

Each leaf a whisper of fun and surprise,
Growing tall tales that tickle the skies.
With every twist, a cheeky boast,
In the jungle of green, they play host to the most.

Shadowed Traditions

In the gloom of the corner, they gather round,
With stories adorned, emitting a sound.
'Remember the day we nearly took flight?'
A talespinning twist under soft moonlight.

Each frond an heirloom with giggles to share,
From distant roots, they twirl with flair.
They sip on the sunlight, bask in delight,
Forging bonds in shadows, where memories ignite.

Verdant Whispers

In a jungle of houseplants, I try to hide,
I swear they gossip, just can't abide.
The leaves all shiver, they share a laugh,
I'm their trusty gardener, but am I their staff?

Each morning I water, they dance in delight,
I trip on their roots, oh what a sight!
They rustle and chuckle, in shades of green,
A leafy conspiracy, I know what they mean.

Treasuring Leafy Legacies

I've a pot of foliage, a real claim to fame,
With more than a few stems, it's quite the game.
Each leaf tells a story, from misdeed to slip,
Like how I forgot, and they dipped down to sip.

A rogue leaf grows wild, with a mind of its own,
It plots to take over, at least that's my tone!
I'll cut it back gently, but it just won't budge,
Who knew such a green could hold such a grudge?

Nature's Tender Embrace

In the heart of my room, a plant gives me cheer,
With such giant leaves, it's like having a peer.
We chat in the morning, in our goofy way,
While I sip my coffee, it laughs through the day.

Its arms stretch so wide, it's a hug in disguise,
Each leaf a reminder of nature's big sighs.
I tell it my secrets, it listens quite well,
And when it tips over, it's my plant-fail tale.

Tendrils of Thought

Around my room, those tendrils roam free,
Like they're whispering secrets, just between you and me.

I've caught them plotting a takeover of sorts,
With a leaf here and there, their pals the reports.

They twist and they curl, in the sun's glowing haze,
Creating a jungle, a leafy maze.
I trip on their mischief, but laugh as I fall,
For in this green chaos, I'm having a ball.

An Ethereal Canopy

In the jungle gym of leaves,
I once lost my favorite sock.
The vines would giggle and tease,
As I danced around the clock.

A squirrel sat, munching on pears,
Declaring himself the king of green.
Swaying gently without cares,
In his court of foliage unseen.

The sunbeams played peek-a-boo,
With shadows that started to prance.
I joined in with the leafy crew,
As we all twirled in a trance.

Caterpillars wore tiny hats,
While crickets composed silly songs.
Nature's party, where laughter chats,
In this realm where everyone belongs.

A Sylvan Retrospective

Once I tried to hug a tree,
That giggled and swayed in reply.
"Don't squeeze too tight!" said a bee,
As he buzzed happily by.

The petals had secrets to spill,
Each flower an odd little friend.
They whispered of wild herbivore thrill,
As I tried to blend in, pretend.

Lizards posed for a group shot,
Wearing sunglasses and hats on their heads.
Their poses were silly, quite the lot,
As laughter spilled over the threads.

Even the ants threw a rave,
With disco lights from the moon above.
In this grove, we all learned to behave,
Frolicking in nature, full of love.

Botanical Reveries

In the garden of funny sights,
Where flowers wear shoes and dance.
With sun-soaked days and starry nights,
Everything here is a bit of a chance.

A gnome with a pipe took a leap,
Into a pot of blooming joy!
The petals began to giggle and peep,
As dreams sprouted from every toy.

Frogs posed as sages on lilypads,
With wisdom that made little sense.
The butterflies flew in their fads,
In this realm, laughter's immense.

In this green field of wild delight,
Where quirkiness finds its sweet blend,
Nature laughs beneath the starlight,
And becomes the most playful friend.

Green Dimensions

Wandering through the leafy maze,
I tripped over a stubborn root.
A plant chuckled in leafy praise,
As my journey turned into a hoot.

The mushrooms wore polka dots bright,
As squirrels hosted tea with the sun.
The toadstools clapped, oh what a sight!
Underneath the green dimension fun.

A whirlwind of petals danced and swayed,
A parade of colors so sublime.
With every giggle, every charade,
Nature's humor ticked like a rhyme.

Each step a bounce, each laugh a cheer,
In this garden where joy transcends.
The green world whispers without fear,
As all of nature joyfully blends.

The Leaf Collector's Tale

In a corner of the room, they thrive,
Potted wonders come alive.
Peeking through the window's gaze,
They dance in sunlight, bright and gay.

One fell leaf, a glorious sight,
I chased it down with all my might.
It slipped and slid across the floor,
Laughed at my antics; oh, what a score!

Gathering greens, a quirky quest,
Each frond a treasure, I confess.
Like a dragonfly on a spree,
Collecting leaves just fills with glee.

At parties, they're the life and star,
Telling tales of where they are.
With every glance, a chuckle shared,
In this leafy world, adventures bared.

Vitality in Green Shades

In the jungle of my living room,
Lurks a plant that makes me zoom.
With leafy limbs in vibrant hues,
It offers plenty of funny views.

A drink of water, a chat, a grin,
As if it's winking, let the fun begin!
Each sprinkle of light, it waves hello,
More vibrant than my last dance show.

In every pot, a vibrant tale,
Of mishaps and spills that never pale.
Bamboo sticks like javelins stand,
Guarding green warriors, oh so grand.

So here's to laughter, growth and cheer,
With every leaf, a memory near.
A rendezvous of plants and glee,
In this green world, we roam so free.

Fronds of Forever

Amid the chaos of my cluttered space,
A leafy friend seems out of place.
Waving fronds, it takes the stage,
A comic actor, full of rage!

Each bend and twist, a funny affair,
Like a comedy show, with flair!
It steals my snacks, my sunny lunch,
A feral plant with a hungry crunch.

In the quiet, it softly sighs,
"A little water, then I'll rise!"
With every joke, a wink and nudge,
Whispering secrets that life won't judge.

Forever green, a comedian true,
In its leafy world, I join the crew.
Together we laugh, through thick and thin,
Creating memories that never wear thin.

Green Time Capsules

Nestled in sunlight, a green delight,
My leafy buddy, quite the sight.
Each new leaf, a story to share,
Like time capsules floating in the air.

Last week's water, spills and thrills,
Harvesting fronds, an art that fills.
I swear it's plotting, oh what a tease,
Making me giggle, down on my knees.

With every curl, it rolls its eyes,
In darkened corners, it cleverly lies.
"Feed me your snacks, let's make a deal,
I promise to charm and never squeal!"

So here we sit, a duo bright,
In this greenery, there's pure delight.
Sharing laughter, growing old,
In living memories, our stories told.

Reflections in the Green Mirror

In the pot, a giant greets,
With holes like Swiss cheese treats.
A leaf says, 'Do I look alright?'
'You're fabulous!' says the light.

Bouncing shadows on the wall,
Giggling plants having a ball.
A whisper floats through the air,
'Is that a bug? Or just my hair?'

Sunlight dances on the floor,
While vines play hide and seek galore.
Each leaf with stories to tell,
Of mishaps in the bug hotel.

When storms blow and rain pours down,
The leaves wave high, don't wear a frown.
They shriek with laughter, drink it in,
With every drop, their tales begin.

The Haunting of Leafy Liaisons

Among the fronds, whispers red,
'Why's the cat still on my bed?'
A ghostly leaf in evening light,
Claims it saw a ghostly sight.

Chasing dust bunnies on the floor,
A saga found by the door.
'Those curtains move, I swear it's true!'
But really, it's just the cat's view.

A ghoulish potted plant does sigh,
'Why do all my neighbors lie?'
They say I'm cursed, but I just blush,
Waiting for the next big rush.

Umbrella ferns form a pact,
To scare the pests, that's a fact.
With devilish smirks and leafed-out pride,
They toss the bugs out for a ride!

When the Garden Remembers

In a nook where secrets sleep,
Lie tales the blossoms always keep.
Each petal feels like an old friend,
Treasure thoughts without an end.

The sunbeam's glow hits just right,
Calling blooms to join the fight.
Together they giggle and sway,
As memories come out to play.

In this garden, time stands still,
Where earthworms wiggle, and blooms thrill.
A chorus of roots sings low,
Of all the seasons 'fore the snow.

With every stir of the gentle breeze,
They spin shared tales with perfect ease.
In a world where joy runs deep,
These garden ghosts will always leap.

Growth Amidst Fading Light

In twilight's glow, the leaves conspire,
Hatching plans with giggles dire.
'Let's stretch over here, then there,'
'We'll catch that light with flair!'

Whispering vines twine around,
Helping each other, love profound.
'You're drooping down, but that's okay,'
'Just pretend it's a leafy spray!'

When petals curl with sunset calls,
The garden sings its mighty thralls.
Each growl of wind, a game they play,
Laughing as night steals the day.

With clinks of pots and rattles deep,
They huddle close, not one to weep.
In shadowed corners, joy ignites,
As they dance in fading lights.

Emerald Echoes of the Past

When I was young, a plant so bright,
It stole the show, a leafy fright.
Its leaves, they spread, a charming way,
I hid behind them when I played.

A friend once said, with a sly grin,
"That beast will eat your socks, come in!"
We chuckled hard as it grew tall,
A household pet that delighted all.

We'd play dress-up with its green gowns,
Creating looks like leafy clowns.
Who knew a plant could harbor such fun,
A botanical friend, second to none?

Years have passed, and here I stand,
With memories of my leafy band.
Though time has flown and youth has slipped,
I smile at those leaves, forever equipped.

Shadows of Leafy Whispers

In the corner where the shadows play,
A giant leaf steals the light of day.
It rustles softly, as if to tease,
"Come taste the joy among the leaves!"

I often find it creeping near,
Adding humor to my daily cheer.
As I sip tea, it winks at me,
"Why not wear a leaf? Just wait and see!"

With silly pranks and leafy jokes,
This plant's the star in all my folks.
Its vines entwine like playful snakes,
Creating laughter with my mistakes.

In every twist, a story we weave,
A comedy rooted in what we believe.
So here's to the green with joyous cheer,
In leafy whispers, laughter's near!

The Dance of Sunlit Green

In morning light, the leaves take flight,
They shimmy, shake, a glorious sight.
With sunlight streaming, they seem to prance,
I swear I caught them in a dance!

With petal twirls and sunlight beams,
They laugh at all my silly dreams.
"Oh, stay awhile!" they seem to call,
As I sip my drink, I smile and sprawl.

The neighbors peek with furrowed brows,
Convinced my plants have made a vow.
Yet here I sit, a hit, a miss,
In this leafy ballroom, pure bliss!

So let them dance, in green delight,
These banter-loving leaves so bright.
For who needs partners, with leaves so keen?
We'll throw a party, my garden's scene!

Fragments of Nature's Heart

In my home, a green confetti fall,
A thousand stories among the thrall.
They've heard my secrets, my hopes and fears,
These leafy fragments hold all my years.

Late-night talks and midnight snacks,
With leafy friends, I've plodded tracks.
"You're just a plant!" I often grumble,
Yet they respond in laughter's tumble.

With every sip of morning brew,
I share my tales, they listen too.
In vibrant hues and glossy sheen,
They keep my dreams, my in-between.

So here's to fragments of joy so bold,
In leafy whispers, my life unfolds.
They may just sit, yet here's the catch:
In every leaf, there's love to match.

Nature's Nostalgia

A leaf grew tall and swayed,
It whispered tales of sunlight played.
Coffee spills and laughter shared,
A jungle gym that none prepared.

In the living room it danced,
While furry friends took a chance.
A face of green, so full of cheer,
It knew our secrets, oh so dear.

Dust bunnies tangled in its vines,
And smudges from those silly times.
When snacks turned into leafy foes,
Our story's where the fun still grows.

Captured in Chlorophyll

A snapshot of a leaf so wide,
Caught hapless crumbs that we would hide.
It stole the show in every game,
For fame was always its true aim.

Silly selfies with this grand plant,
Shadows twirled to a leafy chant.
Vines wore glasses, took a stance,
Competing hard in this green dance.

Dressed with friends in pots so round,
It claimed the throne where joy was found.
With every petal, a laugh to share,
Captured moments, beyond compare.

Hidden in Monochrome Green

In a world of shades, it shines so bright,
Stretched and bent, a funny sight.
It wore a hat made from old socks,
And danced around like silly clocks.

Hiding treats in its green embrace,
Who knew life had such a pace?
With hidden snacks and giggles galore,
A plant with legends waiting to explore.

Sneaky leaves would steal our snacks,
In the night, it held the tracks.
Giggling softly to shades unseen,
In its heart, the laughter gleaned.

Evocative Blooms

Petals in pockets, greens so bold,
Each twist and turn, a story told.
With friends that wore plant hats for fun,
In this green world, we always run.

Chasing shadows, sips in hand,
Laughter stitched, as we all stand.
Snakes took on a whole new flair,
When dancing with this leafy heir.

In sticky summers, it bloomed with pride,
As we sipped tea with sweets inside.
Every sprout a playful tease,
In the light, we found our ease.

Remnants of Eden

In the jungle of my mind, petals dance,
Lurking vines, taking a chance.
Coconuts giggle; lizards tease,
With every twist, I lose my keys.

The fruits debate who's more divine,
While butterflies sip fruit punch wine.
Trees wear hats from last year's fair,
It's a costume party, plants everywhere.

Chasing shadows of childhood days,
Where leaves wore sneakers in playful ways.
I bump my nose into a pot,
Oops! It's a cactus! Oh, what a spot!

The potted pals gossip at dusk,
About how my plants just love to fuss.
Laughter echoes in green retreat,
Where memories bloom, quite bittersweet.

The Leafy Archive

Beneath the soil, secrets lie,
The earthworms smile as they pass by.
Old ferns share tales of days gone by,
When daisies ruled and roses would cry.

The cacti sing their prickly song,
Reminding everyone that life's not wrong.
Even the weeds have stories to tell,
Of forgotten dreams that bloomed so well.

One leaf held up a lost old shoe,
With mossy jokes that nobody knew.
Lemon trees laugh at their own sour fate,
While avocados lament their late date.

In this green vault, hilarity reigns,
With tangled roots and silly chains.
The laughter grows as the sunlight fades,
In the leafy archive, joy cascades.

Lush Chronicles

Once in a garden, I lost my way,
The sunflowers mocked, 'What's wrong today?'
A beetle in glasses read out loud,
The plot of vines, and they were proud.

Squirrels rehearsed for a role in a play,
While daisies danced without delay.
A tomato screamed, 'I'm ripening fast!'
While lettuce sighed, 'Why am I last?'

Twirling in colors, the flowers cheered,
While stinging nettles got a bit weirded.
Chasing each other in wild delight,
Leafy shenanigans filled the night.

In the lush chronicles, mirth takes root,
As seedlings plot with their tiny loot.
The world spins round, in nature's jest,
Where every plant thinks it's the best.

Seasons of the Heart

In spring, the petunias plot a prank,
They swapped the words 'thanks' and 'rank.'
The daisies snicker, "We saw that scene,"
Oh, how the garden thrives in green!

Summer sings of lazy bliss,
When bees start dancing and plants kiss.
A sunflower winks, but oh my dear,
'Bees are my type,' she whispers near.

Autumn comes in with a grand parade,
The pumpkins joke, 'We're not afraid.'
They roll in style, with flare and grace,
While acorns giggle at the race.

Winter arrives, so cold but clear,
With frosty plants spreading good cheer.
In every season, laughter grows,
In the heart's garden, joy overflows.

Enchanted Foliage

Leaves like stars in bright green glow,
Whispers of secrets they might know,
A shadowy throne where cats might plot,
Beneath the leaves, what mischief's wrought?

A dance of shadows on the wall,
Silhouettes of creatures, large and small,
My plants throw parties when I'm away,
I swear I heard them laugh today!

In the corners, they thrive and sprawl,
Crowned with dust bunnies, they stand tall,
Nature's comedians in quiet grace,
Holding court in their leafy space.

So here's to the plants, with humor refined,
In their lush embrace, my joys aligned,
If only they could talk and tease,
I'd laugh until I'm weak at the knees.

Swaying to the Past

As I stroll through the greenery dense,
I find myself lost in their sense,
Each leaf a memory, soft and sweet,
Like old friends gathered, they can't be beat.

They sway in rhythm, a gentle jig,
In this jungle space, life feels big,
Ferns recall tales of mess and fun,
When ice cream dripped in the summer sun.

Echoes of laughter float through the air,
As vines weave stories, a tease, a dare,
With nature's humor, they keep me bright,
In their leafy world, everything's right.

So here's to the plants and their silly charms,
Wrapping my heart with their leafy arms,
Swaying to echoes of laughter past,
In this green kingdom, my joys are vast.

Dancing with Ferns

Ferns pirouette with mirth in their stance,
I join their waltz, lost in a trance,
We twirl with laughter, our spirits high,
In this floral ballroom, time flutters by.

Potting soil shoes and leafy attire,
We dance under sunbeams, fueled by desire,
A couple of potted pals on the roam,
Bringing the fun back into our home.

Each twist and turn, a giggle or two,
With every bounce, my joy feels new,
The plants play tricks, I can't help but grin,
A masquerade ball where no one can win.

So let's dance forever, my leafy friends,
In this joyous party, where laughter transcends,
Dancing with ferns, my heart's light as air,
In our green valhalla, without a care.

Chronicles of the Climbing Plant

In a world where green climbs high and proud,
A tale unfolds that's cheeky and loud,
The winding vines weave stories in jest,
As they venture forth, never a rest.

They conquer the shelves, a daring ascent,
With leaves that ponder, 'Where's the next bent?'
Unfurling their dreams, one vine at a time,
A botanical saga, a hilarious crime.

Sketchy adventures under the lights,
These leafy rebels embracing their nights,
With flickering shadows and giggling greens,
Climbing towards mischief, whatever that means.

So here's to their tales of daring and bliss,
In their green heart, there's humor amiss,
The chronicles whispered by plants so sly,
In laughter and love, we all reach for the sky.

The Legacy of Lushness

In a pot, you wobbled, oh so spry,
Leaves like hands waving, reaching the sky.
But one twisted stem, just too much glee,
You danced on the shelf like you owned the spree.

A sip of your water, a splash on the floor,
We laughed as you dripped, our plant doing more.
Your roots took a trip—adventures so grand,
Yet here you remain, in this funky land.

Muffled giggles echo, trunks hold their breath,
As potted giants plot mischief, no death.
You've tangled my heart with your vibrant hue,
Oh legacy leafy, I'm stuck here with you.

On birthday cakes, you cast your green shade,
Noticing the crumbs where your leaves have played.
A legacy lush—in soil we confide,
Forever you revel, there's nothing to hide.

Dancing in the Botanical Breeze

With a wiggle and wave, you come alive,
Each leaf a dancer, oh how you thrive!
Breezes tickle, they push and they pull,
You twirl to the rhythm, entirely full.

Sipping on sunshine, you're quite the sight,
In the air of the room, what a delightful fright!
When friends visit, they giggle and tease,
'That plant seems to move!'—Oh, it's not just a breeze!

Petals of laughter, you sway with the tune,
Flirting with shadows beneath the bright moon.
How magical moments spread joy through the leaves,
You're the quirky heart—what a plant that believes!

Cherishing the days, outfits of green,
A playful reminder of giggles unseen.
Dancing through life, in the sun's embrace,
You waltz through the chaos with nature's grace!

Nostalgic Tendrils of Time

In the corners of rooms where the stories reside,
Your vines creep like tales, a greenish tide.
Remembering moments of laughter and cheer,
Each leaf a chapter, a memory dear.

Oh, those pranks gone wrong with that watering can,
You soaked my old socks—now I'm a wet fan!
We'd argue and joke, who gave you a sprout?
Turns out, my wild heart didn't care about out!

Time spins like your vines, in whimsical loops,
Growing old together, and now look at us, groups!
Framed in the sunlight, we bask in the glow,
The plant pals we've made, growing slow but sure.

So here's to our journey, a tangled delight,
With tendrils of laughter that reach to the night.
You give me your shade, I'll share all my rhyme,
In this garden we built, the essence of time.

Passages Through the Verdant Wild

In the jungle of my room, adventures commence,
You lead me through forests, wildly intense.
Each leaf a compass, each twist a new trail,
Where laughter and roots weave a wondrous tale.

Forget your GPS, it's damp and it's green,
I'm lost in the foliage, a curious scene.
Armed with a spoon, I venture to prune,
But you elude me, oh sly leafy boon!

Ducking and diving, down the winding path,
You tease and you tickle, instigating my laugh.
Together we roam, through sunshine and shade,
In this verdant wild, our bond is well-made.

So playfully tangled, we'll dance on the edge,
As memories flourish, there's life to allege.
Your vibrant embrace is a ride steeped in styles,
As I wander through life with you—my green smiles.

When Foliage Remembers

In a pot, she sways with grace,
Her leaves recall that wild race.
Chasing sunlight, dodging shade,
Oh, the funny mess we made!

Branching out, she forms a crew,
Each leaf a tale, each tendril new.
They gossip about the gardener's fuss,
Trying to find the perfect bus!

With a twist, they poke their friends,
Bumping each other till it ends.
"Oh no, not that spot!" they giggle and sing,
In this houseplant kingdom, joy's the king!

And when the water drips like rain,
They splash around, forgetting pain.
Each droplet holds a little cheer,
A party hosted without any fear!

Secrets in Each Vein

In the quiet of the night,
Leaves whisper secrets, what a sight!
Stories woven through each streak,
Tickling laughter, oh so cheek!

Look closely, what do you see?
A tiny critter, sipping tea!
With every sip, a tale unfolds,
About mischief, brave and bold.

Tangled tales of garden fame,
Fruits of labor, never the same.
"It was I who ate the crumbs!"
Leaves giggle, feeling quite like chums.

Every vein a bridge to a laugh,
Charting paths on their leafy graph.
In this green world, all's a jest,
Join the fun, you'll feel blessed!

A Tapestry of Splotched Dreams

With splotches here and splashes there,
Leaves dance around without a care.
Each spot a dream, each patch a tale,
Winding through where whims prevail.

Patterns mimicking a wild spree,
Moments stitched with glee, you see!
"Who spilled the paint?" they giggle loud,
"That's our story, let's share it proud!"

In the breeze, they sway and twirl,
Claiming dreams as they whirl.
Sprouting laughter in the air,
What a riot, they can declare!

A delightful mess, this leafy art,
With every splotch, they steal a heart.
Join their canvas, color your scheme,
In this garden, laugh and dream!

Roots of Yesterday's Laughter

Deep below, the roots will jest,
Sharing tales of the leafy quest.
"Oh, remember when we slipped?"
With a chuckle, the foundation flipped.

In the soil, they crack a joke,
Whispered tales beneath the oak.
"Let's dig deeper, find some gold!"
Their giggles spread, warm and bold.

Wiggly tangles, a playful crew,
Growing bonds like morning dew.
They poke through earth, a silly troupe,
As soil dances to their loop!

Festivities bloom, roots sway in cheer,
Every hidden laugh draws us near.
Beneath the surface, joy's the truth,
In roots where echoes of laughter soothe!

A Story Crafted in Chlorophyll

Once a plant stretched high and wide,
Its leaves were bold, with arms spread wide.
It caught the sun, oh what a sight,
But don't ask it to join a fight!

One day it sneezed a leaf or two,
And friends all laughed, 'What's wrong with you?'
It tried to dance, but oh so clumsy,
The cat just sighed, a bit too grumpy.

A party planned, the plants held tight,
But only ferns knew how to write.
They rhymed and swayed, with roots in dirt,
While cacti pricked up, feeling hurt.

But laughter bloomed in every nook,
With tales shared over a good book.
For leafy giants know the game,
A funny plot we can all tame.

Underneath the Green Embrace

In a jungle where the sun shone bright,
A fig tree wore a leaf as a kite.
It flapped and danced, the birds took flight,
And squirrels laughed at such a sight.

'Oh look!', said one, 'It's flying high!'
The tree just mumbled, 'Well, oh my!'
But roots said, 'Stay, don't be so mean!'
They giggled 'neath the leafy green.

The vines entwined in silly games,
With whispers shared, they posed in frames.
Each leaf with secrets, tales to tell,
And laughter wrapped them like a shell.

Their shadows cast, a green parade,
Underneath their leafy jade.
They shared a chuckle, free and grand,
For in plants' hearts, it's all well planned!

Leafy Echoes

In the garden where the green things play,
A leafy friend forgot his way.
He wandered round, with a goofy grin,
And tripped on roots, now where to begin?

The daisies laughed, they bloomed with glee,
'Oh silly plant, come dance with me!'
But every step was quite a mess,
Yet still he twirled in happiness.

Behind the trees a frog did peek,
He croaked so loud, filled with critique.
But lots of giggles filled the air,
As petals swayed, without a care.

Echoes whispered from leaf to leaf,
In joy they found relief from grief.
For each mishap was a tale anew,
In the garden, laughter always grew.

Whispers in the Green

Beneath a vine so sheltering wide,
A secret couple planned a ride.
They tangled roots, the vines entwined,
And left behind a leafy kind.

As rabbits hopped, they joined the fun,
With busy tails, they tried to run.
They danced around like foolish sprites,
Enchanted by the starry nights.

But then a gust blew leaves around,
The laughter echoed, a silly sound.
'The wind escapes with all my notes!'
The plants just giggled, with glee like goats.

So in this space, the green delight,
They've made a pact to share the light.
For every whisper on the breeze,
Turns into laughter, just as it pleased.

Lush Recollections

In a jungle of green, I found a surprise,
A plant with a grin and curious eyes.
It whispered my secrets, oh how it laughed,
With every bold leaf, a memory crafted.

We danced in the sun, around pots of clay,
Each watering can felt like a fun play.
With soil on my shoes and a hat cocked askew,
Those leaves told tales of the wild and the true.

When friends came to visit, they'd poke their heads near,
"Is that a pet?" they'd ask, full of cheer.
I'd chuckle and nod, quite the botanical jest,
For this leafy companion, I loved the best.

Now I sit with my friend, a jungle in tow,
Recalling our journeys, both high and low.
With a wink and a sway, it guides me anew,
In this dance of retreat, life feels like a zoo.

The Garden of Yesterday

In the garden of yonder, I played with a vine,
That curved like a ribbon, oh how it did shine!
We plotted in whispers, the plants and I,
To grow a green fortress that touched the sky.

The daisies were cheeky, the daisies are bold,
They told me of stories that never grow old.
With petals like hats, they'd dance in a row,
While I told the tales of the plants down below.

A fern did a shimmy, just to impress,
While the beans giggled loudly, causing a mess.
With a wink and a nod, the carrots would say,
"Join our potluck; we'll steal the whole day!"

Memories linger, like the scent of the earth,
Each sprout gave a chuckle, each bloom gave a mirth.
With laughter still echoing beneath leafy skies,
In the garden of yesterday, joy never dies.

Nature's Tapestry

In a fabric of plants, in hues bright and bold,
A patchwork of wonders, just waiting to unfold.
With stitches of sunlight and threads of the night,
Each leaf tells a story, each bud holds a light.

The daisies declare, with a wink and a fun,
"We're the stars of this show, now let's make it run!"
The hedges just snicker, in laughter they sway,
As the blooms burst to life, in a colorful ballet.

The cacti look serious, with prickles to spare,
But inside they giggle—just check if you dare!
While robins debate on the best song to sing,
Each note hangs like petals upon drifty wing.

So let's stitch our moments with joy and with cheer,
In a tapestry woven with laughter sincere.
For life's playful dance, in the green and the fair,
Is a celebration, where memories flare.

Flourishing Fragments

In a pot full of laughter, where memories sprout,
Each leaf is a story, without a doubt.
With roots deep in humor, and vines full of fun,
We gather our stories 'neath warm, glowing sun.

A rogue little sprout took a leap for some light,
"Watch me unfold, I'm the star of the night!"
The herbs rolled their eyes, with a sarcastic cheer,
As the tamest of plants fought to conquer their fear.

With branches that reach for the moon up above,
Each blossom declares, "Oh, the joy of love!"
In this quirky green club, where hilarity grows,
Where laughter and wit are the soil that it knows.

So here's to the fragments of flourishing joy,
A jungle of whimsy, oh boy! Oh boy!
Let's plant more memories, in sunlight and shade,
In this garden of giggles, no moment's delayed.

Roots of Remembrance

In a pot so snug and tight,
Lurks a leaf with quite a bite.
It shares tales of snack time woes,
When it grew too high, nobody knows.

The soil whispers secrets low,
Of mischief done by little Joe.
Sneaked a slice of pizza, oh dear,
The plant just giggled, no need to fear.

Poking fun from every stem,
It knows our lives like a dear friend.
With roots entwined in cheerful jest,
It laughs at all our silly quests.

Now we dance around the base,
Swapping stories in this space.
Each leaf a witness to our fun,
Oh, what a life for everyone!

Secrets Beneath the Fronds

Underneath the leafy green,
A treasure trove of things unseen.
Forgotten socks and toy trains too,
In the jungle, we find a shoe!

The frond's a canopy for dreams,
Where laughter hides and sunlight beams.
Under the shade, we tell tall tales,
Of pirate ships and ghostly gales.

Peeking out between the leaves,
A gnome grins — oh, what a tease!
He guards our laughter, keeps it safe,
As we trip over our own waif.

Beneath the fronds, the antics play,
Time stands still in wild array.
While nature giggles, we will sing,
Ever hidden, the joys we bring!

A Tangle of Time

In a twisty vine, we find our pace,
A dance of leaves, a lively space.
We trip and stumble, oh what fun,
In this maze, we're never done.

Each loop a memory, bright and bold,
Of socks played catch in days of old.
With roots that wrap, we spin and sway,
Untangling laughter, come what may.

A tangle of petals, bright and spry,
Whispers secrets as we fly.
To chase the sun, to dodge the rain,
In this adventure, there's no pain.

So let's get lost in endless play,
Where time unwinds, and colors sway.
With every twist, our joy will climb,
In this friendly knot of time!

Sunlight and Shadows

Sunlight dips through leaves so wide,
Where shadows dance, and giggles hide.
Bright rays tickle every nook,
In this habitat, come take a look.

The beam of joy sweeps 'cross the ground,
While playful whispers leap around.
In every shadow, a laugh's refrain,
Oh, the joy of sweet, silly pain!

With a game of tag — who's it now?
The sun peaks in, and we all wow!
Leaves rustle as we make a dash,
Chasing light with a gleeful splash.

So come, bask in the golden glow,
Let shadows wrap you, soft and slow.
In rays of cheer, we spin and sway,
In sunlight's warmth, we find our play!

The Shadow of a Leaf

In the corner it lurks, all green and wide,
Casting shadows where laughter can't hide.
A giant hat on the cat says, 'Look at me!'
As if plants wear hats at a wild jubilee.

With each little tip, it tickles my toes,
A dance of green hands, a whimsical pose.
I swear it just winked, oh what a sight!
This leafy companion, my heart's pure delight.

Sunbeams gather round like a loyal brigade,
While I tell it stories, a masquerade.
And it sways in response, oh what a tease,
A leafy comedian, putting me at ease.

Who knew a plant could have such a grin?
As our friendship grew, I felt it begin.
With every new leaf, we laugh and we sway,
In the shadow of green, we'll play all day.

Nostalgic Canopy

Under a roof of foliage, I reminisce,
There's magic in leaves, a green jungle bliss.
With each rustling sound, I hear echoes of fun,
Oh, to be young again, with mischief undone.

Picnics and laughter in dappled light,
A leafy umbrella, the world's pure delight.
I dared to sneak snacks, oh what a thrill!
While the trees bore witness, they laughed at my skill.

Squirrels joined in with their nutty display,
As birds chirped gossip like they owned the day.
We shared secrets only leaves could keep,
In this canopy high, where wonders run deep.

Now I laugh at the tales beneath the green guise,
Where time skips around, and hilarity flies.
With friends all around, we weave memories bright,
In a nostalgic canopy, forever in sight.

In the Presence of Foliage

Here in the jungle of leaf and light,
A cheeky palm teases my hair with delight.
Plant friends chuckle at my quirky grace,
As I tango with petals in this leafy space.

The ferns start to gossip; oh what a scene,
While cactus grins wide, feeling all green.
I tripped on a vine, oh dear, what a fall!
The plants burst with laughter, it's a grand ball.

Every leaf tells a story, each twist a new tale,
As I pirouette clumsily, dreaming of sails.
In a world that's so leafy, who needs a stage?
The antics of plants can steal any page.

So here's to the foliage, my friends so absurd,
With a wink and a leaf, they whisper a word.
In the presence of green, there's joy to unfold,
In this funny little garden, life never gets old.

Green Tales Untold

Among the tall stalks, a secret does lie,
A story of antics that touch the sky.
Where vines play hopscotch on the warm summer floor,
And leaves burst with laughter, always wanting more.

I found a rogue sprout with a quirk in its style,
Prancing about like a dandelion child.
With each little dance, it calls to the breeze,
As if whispering secrets to the wandering trees.

The pots hold their gossip, each flower in cheer,
Sharing old tales that make me shed a tear.
And when night falls, with the fireflies above,
The plants break into song, a chorus of love.

So here's to the green, the laughter, the play,
With tales untold and mischief at bay.
Each leaf a reminder of joyous delight,
In this whimsical jungle, everything feels right.

Climbing the Walls of Memory

In the corner, a green vine sprawls,
It stretches and creeps up the walls,
Reminds me of parties, laughter loud,
And my cat thinking she's king of the crowd.

A leaf fell down, big as a plate,
I served it to friends, they called it fate,
Chips and dip? No, this is gourmet!
Only the brave munch on foliage buffet!

Memories twist like the roots so thick,
Each party was fun, but a bit of a trick,
I danced with a cactus, oh what a sight,
Just me and my plants, under disco light!

Now those days linger, like soil on a shoe,
Each leaf's a reminder, what silly things we'd do,
With laughter and plants, my heart swells with glee,
Climbing those walls is still fun, you see!

Echoes of the Tropics

Bananas hung low, swaying with grace,
In my head there's a tropical place,
With hula-hoops made of palm fronds,
And pineapple hats that nobody responds.

The parrots squawk, oh what a sight,
They mimic my laugh, yes, they got it right,
We danced on the beach, in flip-flops and bliss,
With a sandwich in hand—a tropical kiss!

Bikini-clad dreams under coconut trees,
But my sunscreen turned an unexpected tease,
Stripes like a zebra, oh what a riot,
And laughter erupted, we just couldn't deny it.

Echoes of fun linger soft in the breeze,
With laughter we danced, like leaves in a tease,
So lift your drinks, toast to the cheer,
In echoes of tropics, we hold them near!

Botanical Footprints

Walking barefoot through the garden path,
I spotted a flower that made me gasp,
A flower with a face, oh what a find,
It winked at me as I stumbled behind.

The footprints we leave, a muddy parade,
From dodging big bees that just won't fade,
We trip on the vines, giggling like kids,
In this jungle of memories, we are the wids!

I chased a butterfly, it laughed in the sun,
It led me to mischief, oh what fun!
With dirt on my nose and petals in hand,
I'll craft these weird stories, they'll always stand.

So here's to the blooms, the smiles and the cheer,
Botanical footprints, let's raise a beer,
With laughter and petals, my heart gives a twirl,
In the garden of memories, life's a wild swirl!

In the Hue of Hostel Gardens

In a hostel garden, plants everywhere,
A cactus named Bob gives me a stare,
While I sip on my drink, he steals the show,
With spines that are sharp, oh dear, take it slow!

Friends gather 'round, in pots we confide,
Each plant has a story, laughter and pride,
A fern found a crush, they sway side by side,
Oh, botanic love, with no need to hide!

Tomatoes and herbs, growing all wild,
While I lost my flip-flop—too bad, I just smiled,
The basil was sad, I'll bring back a friend,
A sock on a plant, that's fashion, my trend!

In the hue of the garden, laughter takes flight,
With stories of plants, and fun every night,
So let's raise our glasses, toast to the green,
In hostel gardens, we're living the dream!

The Memory of a Leafy Embrace

In a jungle of green, I once did prance,
With a plant friend who fancied a dance.
Its leaves waved hello, like hands in the air,
While I stumbled and tripped, without a care.

We'd laugh at the sun, making shadows that play,
As I told it my secrets, in my own silly way.
Its leaves crinkled up as if they might giggle,
While I tossed peanuts, hoping to wiggle.

The local birds chirped, a comedy show,
As I mimicked their calls, putting on quite a glow.
Between sips of nectar, that leafy delight,
We shared jokes that made the moon giggle at night.

Now every green leaf brings a smile to my face,
Remembering dances in our jungle space.
With laughter echoing through branches so wide,
Oh, the silly adventures with my leafy guide!

Recollections in the Canopy

Up high in the branches, my pals had a blast,
We'd swing to the rhythm of the breezy past.
My leafy companion thought it was a game,
Every rustle and shake, a call to the same.

I'd tell it my dreams, to grow tall like a tree,
It'd respond with a wiggle, 'Just cling close to me!'
We'd plot grand adventures, like pirates set sail,
With the sun as our map, and the clouds as our trail.

With raindrops as confetti, we'd throw our own bash,
Dancing under storms, hearing thunderous crash.
The creatures would join, a wild, wacky crew,
Making music from leaves, with a rhythm so true.

Now I look back fondly, at that leafy affair,
Where giggles and sunshine danced in the air.
Each vine holds a story, each leaf a delight,
In the canopy's heart, our memories take flight.

Echoes of Nature's Tenderness

In a garden of chaos, we had our own zone,
With leaves as our curtains, we never felt alone.
I shared a wild sandwich, toasted just right,
While my plant pal sighed, 'Save some for tonight!'

When storms rolled on through, we danced in the rain,
A soggy parade, with mud on the plain.
The neighbors looked puzzled, oh what a sight,
A leafy comedian stole every spotlight!

We'd giggle with crickets, who joined in the cheer,
And play hide-and-seek with the butterflies near.
Oh how we created our whimsical lore,
With tales that made roots giggle and explore.

Now every fond thought blooms with roots so profound,
In the echoes of whispers, where laughter is found.
Nature's own chorus, a tune we still play,
In a garden of memories, where we laughed every day!

Whispers from the Rooted Past

Down in the soil, where secrets like to creep,
Lived a wise old plant that never fell asleep.
With roots intertwined, it whispered to me,
'Life's funny in dirt, just wait and see!'

We traded our stories, as friends do on walks,
While ants held debates over botanical talks.
The worms joined the banter, with tales from below,
In our quirky underground, laughter would flow.

When sunshine arrived, we'd take our parade,
With leaves in the air, no chance to evade.
The flowers would giggle, petals brightly spun,
While we laughed at the antics of the overly fun sun!

Now as I wander through patches of green,
I recall the mischief the garden once seen.
With whispers of joy from roots to the sky,
My trusty green friend still makes me smile high!

www.ingramcontent.com/pod-product-compliance
Lightning Source LLC
Chambersburg PA
CBHW071127130526
44590CB00056B/2837